PowerKids Readers:

MY SCHOOL™

Meet My Teacher

Elizabeth Vogel

The Rosen Publishing Group's
PowerKids Press™
New York

1

Published in 2002 by The Rosen Publishing Group, Inc.
29 East 21st Street, New York, NY 10010

First Edition

Book Design: Michael Donnellan

Photo Credits: all photos by Cindy Reiman except planets photo on page 22 by PhotoDisc.

We extend a special thank-you to Mrs. Padilla and her students at the S.F.B. Morse Child Magnet School in Poughkeepsie, New York for their participation in this project.

Vogel, Elizabeth.
Meet my teacher / Elizabeth Vogel.
    p. cm. — (My school)
Includes bibliographical references (p.   ) and index.
ISBN 0-8239-6032-3 (library binding)
1. Elementary school teachers—Juvenile literature.
[1. Teachers. 2. Occupations.] I. Title.
LB1776 .V64 2002
372.11—dc21

                                          2001000606

Manufactured in the United States of America

2

Contents

3

I am a teacher. I teach children in grade school. My students are in first grade.

Our Solar System

Diary: Froglets

JUNE 15 Today our first froglet came out of the water. It climbed up a stick that we'd put in the fish tank. The froglet looked like a frog but it still had its tail. We called him Fred.

I work in a school that has many classrooms. This is my classroom. This is the blackboard, where I write important things. I use chalk to write on the blackboard.

I decide what lessons to teach my students. I teach many subjects. Some of the subjects that I teach are reading, writing, math, and science.

9

I write in my attendance book. This book has a list of the students in my class. I write down who is here.

I teach reading. We read books like the one you are reading now! We learn new words each day.

Sometimes I read stories or poems to the class. My students are helping me read this story.

We have lunch in the middle of the day. It is important to eat a healthy lunch. A good lunch gives my students energy for the rest of the day. A good lunch helps me, too!

17

In the afternoon, we have a science lesson. Here we are drawing pictures of the Sun, the Moon, and the planets. Tomorrow we will learn about the stars.

19

When the bell rings, I know it is time to go. I make sure the students get home safely. I will see them tomorrow.

Words to Know

attendance book

blackboard

chalk

planets

Here is another book to read about teachers:

Teachers
by Tami Deedrick
Capstone Press

To learn more about teachers, check out this Web site:

http://home.nycap.rr.com/cjem/ems/
    page4.html

Index

Word Count: 218

Note to Librarians, Teachers, and Parents

PowerKids Readers are specially designed to help emergent and beginning readers build their skills in reading for information. Simple vocabulary and concepts are paired with stunning, detailed images from the natural world around them. Readers will respond to written language by linking meaning with their own everyday experiences and observations. Sentences are short and simple, employing a basic vocabulary of sight words, as well as new words that describe objects or processes that take place in the natural world. Large type, clean design, and photographs corresponding directly to the text all help children to decipher meaning. Features such as a contents page, picture glossary, and index help children get the most out of PowerKids Readers. They also introduce children to the basic elements of a book, which they will encounter in their future reading experiences. Lists of related books and Web sites encourage kids to explore other sources and to continue the process of learning.